Once Upon A Quilt

Fairy Tales in Fabric

That Patchwork Place®

Bonnie Kaster and Virginia Athey

Credits

Editor-in-Chief .... Kerry I. Smith
Technical Editor .... Janet White
Managing Editor .... Judy Petry
Copy Editor .... Tina Cook
Proofreaders .... Melissa Riesland, Leslie Phillips
Design Director .... Cheryl Stevenson
Text and Cover Designer .... Amy Shayne
Production Assistant .... Marijane E. Figg
Illustrator .... Laurel Strand
Photographer .... Brent Kane

MISSION STATEMENT

We are dedicated to providing quality products
and service by working together to inspire creativity
and to enrich the lives we touch.

Once upon a Quilt: Fairy Tales in Fabric
© 1997 by Bonnie Kaster and Virginia Athey
That Patchwork Place, Inc., PO Box 118
Bothell, WA 98041-0118 USA

Library of Congress Cataloging-in-Publication Data
Kaster, Bonnie,
    Once upon a quilt : fairy tales in fabric / Bonnie Kaster and
Virginia Athey.
      p. cm.
    ISBN 1–56477–165–2
    1. Appliqué—Patterns. 2. Patchwork—Patterns.
3. Quilting—Patterns. 4. Fairy tales in art. I. Athey, Virginia
II. Title.
TT779.K38 1997
746.46'041—dc21   96–49187
                              CIP

Printed in the United States of America
02 01 00 99 98 97 6 5 4 3 2

Acknowledgments

My thanks to:

My friend and business partner, Virginia Athey. I've included her as my coauthor because she made sense out of my scribblings and notes. She helped me organize my ideas and get them onto the computer disk.

Evergreen Quilters, Green Bay, Wisconsin, whose members have always been eager to see my newest designs.

My special friends Adeline Mong and Rose Baumgartner, who have been like mothers to me when I needed them most.

Mary Jo Gussert, for her excellent quilting skills.

My daughters, Lisa and Shana, who have always been proud of the concoctions I've made for them.

My son, Dean, for his honest and expert opinions.

My wonderful husband and best friend, Paul. His support and great sense of humor have sustained me for thirty-two years.

And you, for purchasing this book. I know that in your heart you still believe fairy tales can come true.

Bonnie Kaster

Table of Contents

Introduction

THE DESIGNS IN this book are interpretations of my favorite fairy tales, myths, and legends. They are all pictorial appliqué wall hangings. Make one for a favorite person in your life: a child or a child at heart.

You can make these quilts as I have designed them or change them to suit yourself. It is much easier to change an appliqué design than a pieced one. For example, if you like the overall Dragonslayer design but don't want the large cloud at the bottom right, you can remove it. The final shape and size of the quilt remain the same. Appliqué is exciting because you can change whatever you don't like about a design and make it your own.

Fabric

FOR QUILTMAKERS these days, choosing fabric can be an overwhelming task. There are small prints, large prints, decorator and dress fabrics, batiks, and tie-dyes. There are marbled, air-brushed, hand-painted, checked, striped, and gilded fabrics. I have a large selection of beautiful prints and hand-dyed fabrics. Some I bought, some I dyed myself, and some were gifts from friends who also dye fabric. Streaked or mottled hand-dyed fabrics work well in both landscape and floral designs.

Before using commercial cotton fabrics, I wash and dry them. Prewashing to remove the sizing makes the fabric more pliable and easier to appliqué and quilt. Hand-dyed fabrics usually have been washed many times, so I don't prewash them.

I use 100% cotton fabric extensively, but not exclusively. When I am looking for a particular color or accent I use other fabrics, such as metallic knits, lightweight decorator fabrics, lightweight corduroy, and rayon challis. Consider the intended use of the finished piece when choosing fabrics other than cotton. For wall hangings, you have freedom to choose unusual fabrics, such as velvets, metallics, and laces, because these quilts will not need frequent cleaning.

You may find a beautiful fabric that incorporates all the colors you love—a floral, stripe, paisley, plaid, or even a decorator print. I call this a "theme" fabric. Study the theme fabric closely and base your palette on its colors. I usually use a theme fabric for the final border of a quilt. Theme fabric can also be used in the pictorial areas of the quilt, as the stem of a flower, a leaf, or the dress of a princess. Using the theme fabric in the body of the quilt as well as in a border unifies the overall color scheme.

For a glittery or shiny accent, use metallic fabric. I particularly like the gold and silver knits available in the fine-fabric sections of fabric stores. Metallic knits are slippery and you can't draw a turn-under line on them, but they appliqué beautifully with only a ³⁄₁₆"-wide seam allowance if you baste the appliqué piece and clip the inner curves.

Another special fabric I often use is Ultra Suede®. Since you don't have to turn under the edges, it works especially well for tiny details that are difficult to appliqué. Cut Ultra Suede to the finished size of the appliqué piece; then stitch with thread that matches the appliqué.

Be careful not to press Ultra Suede or metallic fabrics with a hot iron since they may melt or be otherwise damaged by the heat. You don't have to prewash these fabrics, but they are washable.

Supplies

FREEZER PAPER: I use freezer paper for templates. See "Appliquéing the Pieces" on pages 8–9.

MARKERS: A permanent, fine-line marker works well for drawing details such as eyelashes and spider webs. For shading larger areas, I use markers with medium or wide tips. If you use nonpermanent colored markers, press the marked fabric with a hot iron to set.

NEEDLES: For appliqué, I like a long, very fine needle with a small eye for easy needle turning. Size 11 or 12 Sharps work well. To quilt, I prefer a size 9 or 10 Between. Any thin, long basting needle is good for basting appliqué pieces to the background or basting together the quilt layers before quilting.

PENCILS: I use a No. 2 lead pencil for tracing template patterns onto freezer paper. I prefer a mechanical pencil for tracing around templates on light fabrics because it makes a very fine dark line and never needs sharpening. For tracing on dark fabrics, I like a soft white or silver pencil.

PENS: A retractable ball-point pen is the best tool I've found for transferring dressmaker's carbon to fabric.

PINS: I use very fine, long (1¼"), glass-head pins. They are easy to grasp and slip through fabric easily.

RULERS: Use only good-quality rulers and triangles for accurate measuring and squaring. Each ruler should have clearly marked increments and a 45°-angle mark for mitering.

SCISSORS: Look for a medium size (7") pair of scissors that is comfortable in your hand and makes a sharp cut to the point. Use these scissors exclusively for cutting fabric. Use less expensive scissors for cutting templates.

THREAD: I prefer cotton or cotton-covered polyester thread for appliqué. Silkier threads slip out of my needle too easily. I match the thread color to the appliqué piece, not the background.

General Instructions

THE QUILTS IN this book are made by appliquéing design pieces to a background fabric to form a picture. Each cutting chart calls for a background 1" larger all around than the finished dimensions. You will trim the background to the correct size after the appliqué is complete.

Some of the appliqué backgrounds in this book consist of a sky section and either a water or a land section. Some quilts have clouds or trees that need to be appliquéd to the sky section before being sewn to the land or water. In some cases you can machine stitch background sections together for strength, stability, and ease of construction. Each quilt plan includes specific instructions.

Seven of the ten quilt patterns are on the pullouts at the back of this book. The other three quilt patterns appear in sections on pages 46–66. Trace the pattern sections for these quilts onto a large sheet of paper to construct the full pattern, referring to the accompanying Section Guide. (Because lines may show through from the back of each pullout, you may want to trace even the full-size patterns onto fresh paper to avoid confusion.)

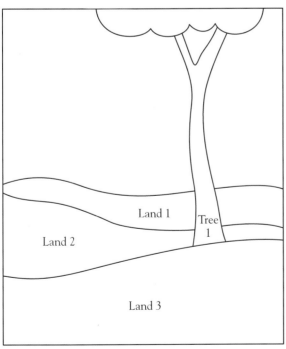

Each quilt plan lists the pieces in the order in which they must be appliquéd. Pay close attention, because tree 1 may need to be appliquéd *after* land 2 and *before* land 3.

Transferring a Design to Background Fabric

For proper placement of appliqué pieces, you need to transfer design lines to the background fabric. Transfer only the outlines needed for placement, and do so lightly. Refer to the pattern and the color photograph for extra guidance. Use the transfer method that works best for you: a light box or window, or dressmaker's carbon.

To trace a pattern using a light box or window:
Fold the background fabric in half and in half again; press. Unfold the background fabric and center the pattern underneath it, matching the fabric creases to the center lines on the pattern.

Lightly mark the pattern's outside edges on the fabric, and then trace placement lines.

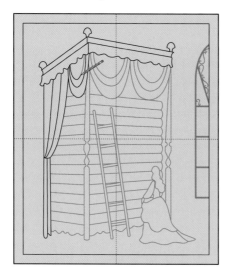

To transfer a pattern using dressmaker's carbon:

Place the dressmaker's carbon, waxed side down, on the right side of the background fabric. Center the pattern right side up on top of both layers; trace placement lines with a ball-point pen.

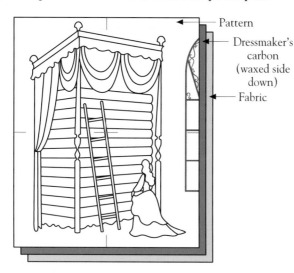

Pattern

Dressmaker's carbon (waxed side down)

Fabric

Appliquéing the Pieces

FREEZER PAPER TEMPLATES

Freezer paper is shiny and waxy on one side and dull on the other. The shiny side sticks to fabric when you press with a hot, dry iron (cotton setting).

To make templates, place freezer paper shiny side down over the pattern and trace each appliqué shape with a pencil. Many templates overlap. Be sure to trace each shape separately. If there are any marks or instructions on the template pattern, transfer these to the template.

Using paper scissors, cut out each template. Press the shiny side of the template to the *right* side of the appliqué fabric. Place curved pieces on the bias. Using the edge of the freezer paper as a guide, trace around each template with a mechanical pencil. This is the turn-under line.

Using fabric scissors, cut out the appliqué pieces, adding a 3/16"-wide seam allowance beyond the edge of the freezer paper. To make sharply curved pieces easier to appliqué, add only a 1/8"-wide seam allowance. Leave the freezer paper on the fabric until you are ready to baste it in place.

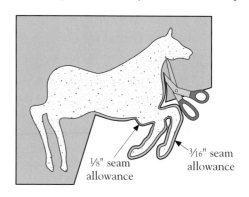

1/8" seam allowance

3/16" seam allowance

TIP

Clip the inner (concave) curves of appliqué pieces to the turn-under line drawn on the fabric (the freezer-paper edge). Your needle can easily sweep these edges under. Never clip outer (convex) curves, or you will end up with points where the curves should be. Appliqué outer curves first, needle-turning carefully. Needle-turn the inner curves last of all.

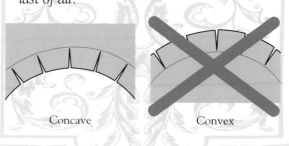

Concave

Convex

BASTING

Few quilters enjoy basting appliqué pieces to the background. However, I have found that the time spent basting saves me time as I appliqué. The basting prevents the appliqué pieces from shifting and allows me to hold the pieces properly for sewing.

To begin, remove the freezer paper from the appliqué pieces. (The freezer paper can be saved to use again if desired.) Arrange and pin the appliqué pieces on the background fabric in the order in which they will be appliquéd. Make sure seam allowances overlap as necessary. Once all the pieces are pinned in place, take a moment to view the design to make sure the colors appeal to you. Now is the time to change appliqué fabrics if any are too bright or the wrong color.

A large spool of white polyester thread works well for basting and lasts a long time. Working with about 18" of thread at a time, take long stitches (½" or so) around each appliqué piece, about ⅜" from the edge. Baste down the middle of long, thin pieces such as branches and stems.

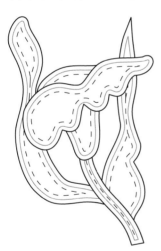

NEEDLE-TURN APPLIQUÉ

Appliqué the pieces to the background in order. As you stitch, roll the seam allowance under with your needle until the pencil line is hidden. Edges that will be covered by other pieces can be left unsewn. In a few places, one piece will lie partly under and partly over another piece. Appliqué the part that goes underneath, leaving the part that will be on top unsewn until the other piece is appliquéd.

Leave forelock unsewn until unicorn is appliquéd.

Appliqué first.

To reduce bulk, carefully trim the background fabric behind the appliqué pieces. For detailed instruction in this technique, refer to *Appliqué in Bloom* by Gabrielle Swain (That Patchwork Place).

MAKING STEMS

Even the smallest bias bar is too wide for the stems in these patterns, so try this method instead. Cut a bias strip of stem fabric the required length and ⅝" to ¾" wide. Carefully press one long edge of the strip under ⅛". Baste the strip to the background fabric.

Appliqué the folded edge to the background. Pull out the basting thread and, using your needle, roll the other edge under and appliqué.

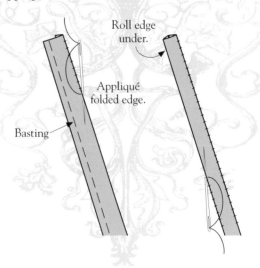

Roll edge under.

Appliqué folded edge.

Basting

Adding Details with Markers

To add details too difficult to appliqué, I enhance fabrics with colored markers. See the fancy grillwork on the window in "The Princess and the Pea" (page 22). Practice using markers on scrap fabric to see what effects you can achieve. Have fun with this technique; it's not as difficult as it may seem.

Once you know what your markers will do, follow the steps below to enhance an appliqué piece.

1. Trace the template onto the uncoated side of a piece of freezer paper. Cut out the template and press the shiny side to the right side of the appliqué fabric. Using a fine-line pencil, trace around the template to mark the turn-under line. Do not cut out the fabric piece.

2. Remove the freezer-paper template. Press a scrap piece of freezer paper larger than the appliqué piece to the *wrong* side of the appliqué fabric. This stabilizes the fabric so it will not roll or move as you mark on it. Using the marker of your choice, carefully draw on the fabric as desired. Remember, it is best to practice on scraps first.

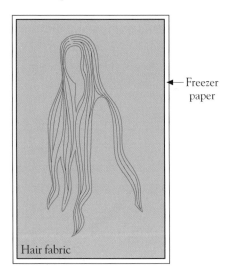

Freezer paper

Hair fabric

3. Remove the freezer paper from the fabric. If necessary, press the appliqué piece with a hot iron to set the markings. Cut out the appliqué piece, adding a 3⁄16"-wide seam allowance. Clip the inner curves and appliqué in place.

Framing a Circular Design

Four of the quilts have a circular design area, which presents some bordering challenges. The easiest way to create a circle within a square or rectangular frame is to use reverse appliqué.

1. Fold the frame fabric in half and in half again; then press with an iron.

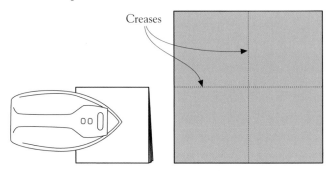

Creases

2. Center the frame fabric, right side up, exactly over the pattern, matching the fabric creases to the center lines on the pattern. Use a pencil to trace the design-area circle onto the right side of the fabric. This is the turn-under line.

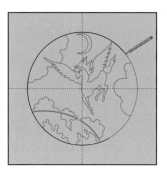

3. Cut out the fabric 1⁄4" inside the pencil line.

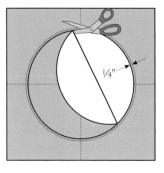

1⁄4"

4. Lay the frame fabric over the appliquéd background fabric, both right sides up. Match and pin the outside edges; then pin all around the circle. Baste the pieces together all around the

circle, ½" from the raw edge; then baste the outside straight edges to keep the fabrics from shifting.

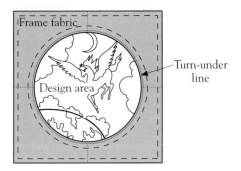

5. Appliqué the frame fabric to the background fabric, turning the circle's edge under just enough so that the pencil line disappears. You may want to clip the circle at 1" intervals to make it easier to turn.

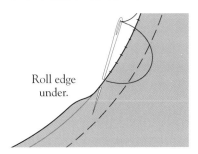

Roll edge under.

Attaching Borders

Borders should complement, not overpower, the center of the quilt. All the quilts in this book are pictures for hanging on walls, so frame them as you would any picture, but with fabric. A narrow (¼"-wide) inner border of a contrasting color defines the center of the quilt. The outside border should incorporate some of the colors in the design area of the quilt. To make the border look like a frame, miter the corners.

BORDERS WITH MITERED CORNERS

1. Determine the outside dimensions of the quilt top, including borders. Cut border strips to these lengths, plus 2" to 3". If the quilt has multiple borders, as all the quilts in this book do, join the strips for each side lengthwise; then stitch the joined strips to the quilt top as a single unit.

2. Mark the centers and finished ends of each side of the quilt top and each border strip. Stitch each border to the quilt top, matching the center and end points.

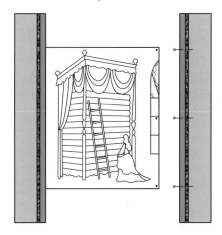

3. Place a corner of the quilt top on your ironing board. Fold one border strip under at a 45° angle. Make sure the seams meet exactly; then pin and press.

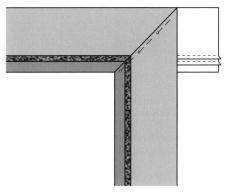

Pin fold with pins pointing outward.

4. Fold the quilt diagonally, right sides together, lining up the edges of the border. Stitch on the pressed crease, sewing from the corner of the quilt top to the outside edge of the border.

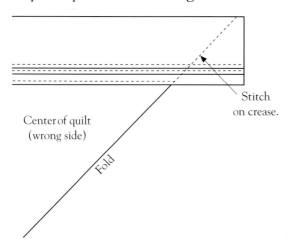

Stitch on crease.

Center of quilt (wrong side)

Fold

5. Press the seam open and trim to a ¼"-wide seam allowance. Repeat with the remaining corners.

BORDERS WITH STRAIGHT-CUT CORNERS

1. Measure the length of the quilt top across the center, and cut border strips to that length. Mark the centers of the quilt top sides and the border strips, and stitch the strips to the sides, matching centers and ends.

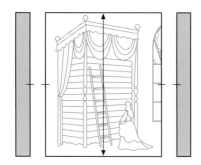

2. Measure the width of the quilt top across the center, including borders, and cut border strips to that length. Mark the centers of the top and bottom edges and the centers of the

border strips. Stitch the strips to the quilt top, matching centers and ends.

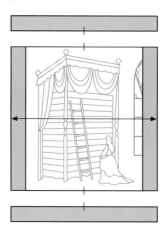

Marking the Quilt Top

After you complete the appliqué and attach the borders, press the quilt top and make sure the outside edges are square. Lightly mark the desired quilting design on the quilt top with a white or silver chalk pencil. I often quilt vertical, horizontal, or diagonal lines in the background. If there is an expanse of sky or water, I use wavy lines to give texture to the water or to mimic clouds in the sky. In addition to quilting on the marked lines to create textures and design details, I usually quilt in-the-ditch around all the appliqué pieces to emphasize them.

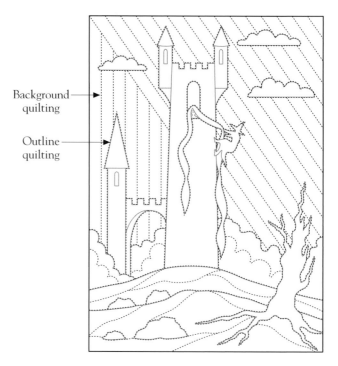

Background quilting

Outline quilting

Basting and Quilting

Each project in this book includes my suggestions for quilting. I chose to quilt the designs simply, using lines to fill the background and simple motifs to suggest waves or flowing clouds, and quilting in-the-ditch to outline objects.

A quilt made with lightweight cotton or polyester batting looks soft but not puffy. Lightweight batting quilts easily and hangs well. Cut the backing fabric and batting 2" larger on each side than the dimensions of the quilt top. Place the backing fabric on your work surface wrong side up, smooth the batting over it, and then carefully center the quilt top on the batting, right side up. Baste the layers together, beginning in the center and working outward. Thread-baste for hand quilting; pin-baste for machine quilting. Begin quilting in the center of the quilt, and then work outward.

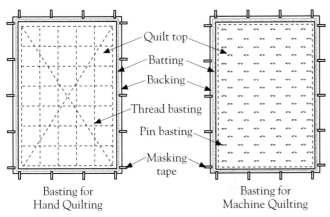

Quilt top
Batting
Backing
Thread basting
Pin basting
Masking tape

Basting for Hand Quilting — Basting for Machine Quilting

Adding a Hanging Sleeve

1. Cut a 3"-wide piece of fabric that equals the finished width of the quilt.
2. Press under ¼" of one long edge. Turn under ½" on each end, turn under ½" again, press, and stitch.
3. Pin the strip to the top edge of the quilt back and bind as usual.
4. Hand stitch the pressed edge of the sleeve to the back as shown.

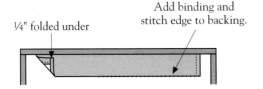

¼" folded under

Add binding and stitch edge to backing.

Binding the Edges

The binding is the final color at the edges of the quilt. I usually use a very dark or a very light binding to provide a defining line. Cut binding on the crosswise grain.

1. Cut a 1¼" wide binding strip for each side of the quilt. If necessary, sew strips together to fit the quilt sides.
2. Fold under one edge of each binding strip ¼" and press.

¼"

3. Sew the binding strip to the sides of the quilt, right sides together, matching the raw edges of the binding strip to the edge of the quilt top and taking a ¼" seam. Trim the binding even with the batting and backing at each end. Fold the binding to the back of the quilt and hand stitch in place.

Quilt front (already quilted)

4. Sew the binding to the top and bottom edges of the quilt. Turn under ¼" at each end; blindstitch the ends closed.

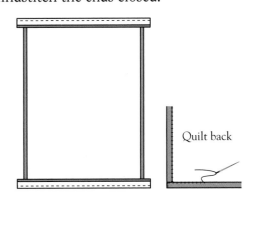

Quilt back

Color and Design

THE COLORS WE use in our quilts generally reflect how we feel about ourselves, the world around us, and of course, the quilt's design. To get started, decide whether your quilt should have "warm" or "cool" colors. These two little words—*warm* and *cool*—can save you hours of planning and choosing fabrics. On an emotional level, warm colors evoke dynamic, exciting, invigorating feelings; cool colors convey calm, restful, peaceful feelings. Once you choose the mood you want your quilt to evoke, you can determine whether you want a predominantly warm or cool color scheme.

Red and yellow are the primary warm colors. Warm palettes can include all shades and tints of red and yellow, including brown, rust, gold, tan, yellow-green, orange, and most earth colors. Blue is the primary cool color. Purple, lavender, orchid, aqua, navy blue, blue-greens, and grays all belong to a cool palette. See the facing page for examples of warm and cool colors.

Keep color and value contrast in mind as you choose fabrics for your quilt. Value (lightness and darkness) can emphasize some elements in a design and make others less important. In a landscape background, keep the values similar to make objects in the distance recede or blend together. Notice the clouds and land in the background of "The Little Mermaid" (page 19). Make foreground objects distinct by using colors and values that contrast with the background. See how the unicorns contrast with the background in "The Unicorns" (page 21).

Warm colors

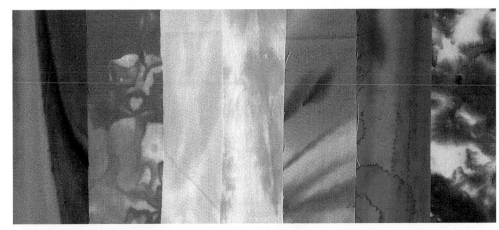

Cool colors

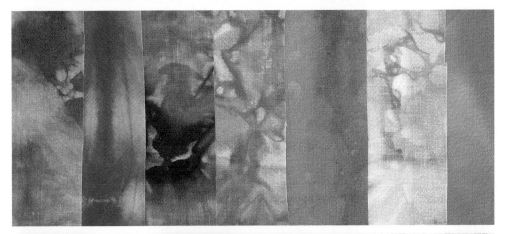

Gallery

Cinderella *by Bonnie Kaster, 1996, DePere, Wisconsin, 39" x 28".*

Pegasus *by Bonnie Kaster, 1996, DePere, Wisconsin, 32" x 32".*

Dragonslayer *by Bonnie Kaster, 1996, DePere, Wisconsin, 26" x 36".*

The Little Mermaid *by Bonnie Kaster, 1996, DePere, Wisconsin, 30" x 35".*

Hansel and Gretel *by Bonnie Kaster, 1996, DePere, Wisconsin, 32" x 27".*

The Unicorns *by Bonnie Kaster, 1996, DePere, Wisconsin, 31" x 31".*

The Princess and the Pea *by Bonnie Kaster, 1996, DePere, Wisconsin, 29" x 33".*

The Ugly Duckling *by Bonnie Kaster, 1996, DePere, Wisconsin, 33" x 33".*

Rapunzel *by Bonnie Kaster, 1996, DePere, Wisconsin, 28" x 36".*

Thumbelina *by Bonnie Kaster, 1996, DePere, Wisconsin, 31" x 31".*

THEN HER GODMOTHER commanded her above all things not to stay after midnight, telling
her that–if she stayed one moment later–the coach would be a pumpkin again, her horses mice,
her coachman a rat, her footmen lizards and her clothes would become just as they were before.

Charles Perrault † *Cinderella*

Cinderella

**Finished
size
39" x 28"**

**Color
photo
page 16**

MATERIALS

Fabric (44" wide)	Pieces to Cut	Fabric (44" wide)	Pieces to Cut
⅝ yd. dark blue	15" x 31" sky	Assorted scraps	Castle 2, 4, 6, 8–10*, 12, 14, 16, 18, underskirt, Cinderella body, hair, arms 1 & 2, sash, bow, ribbons 1 & 2, sleeves 1 & 2, land 1 & 2, stair side strip
⅜ yd. blue print	7" x 31" foreground		
¼ yd. mottled dark blue	Clouds 1–4		
¼ yd. *each* of 4 greens	Trees 1 & 2, bushes 1–3		
¼ yd. *each* of 6 purples	Castle 1, 3, 5, 7, 11, 13, 15, steps 1–7	¼ yd. for first border	4 strips, each ¾" x 42"
¼ yd. off-white print	Coach 1–5, wheels	⅝ yd. for second border	4 strips, each 5" x 42"
¼ yd. gold metallic	Coach trim 1–9	1½ yds. for backing and binding	
¼ yd. light pink	Bodice & skirt	43" x 32" piece of batting	
9" x 12" light yellow	Moon, castle 17	*Ultra Suede optional	

Instructions

Referring to "Appliquéing the Pieces" on pages 8–9, prepare the templates and appliqué pieces using the pullout pattern.

1. Sew the sky and foreground fabrics together along the 31"-long edges using a ¼"-wide seam allowance. Press the seam toward the foreground.

2. Fold the sky/foreground piece in half and in half again; then press gently to mark the center. Unfold the fabric and align the creases with the center lines on the pattern. Transfer pattern lines to the background piece for appliqué placement.

3. Appliqué the pieces to the background in the following order:
   Bush 1, land 1, bush 2, land 2, bush 3
   Moon, clouds 1–4
   Castle 1–18
   Steps 1–7 (You can strip piece stairs to-gether, arranging the values from dark at the bottom to light at the top, before appliquéing to the background.)
   Stair side strip
   Trees 1 and 2
   Cinderella body, hair, arm 1, sleeve 1, bodice, arm 2, sleeve 2, underskirt, skirt, ribbons 1 and 2, sash, bow
   Coach trim 1, coach 1 and 2, trim 2, coach 3–5 (The coach windows must be reverse appliquéd to let the background show through.)
   Trim 6
   Spokes, wheel rims, trim 7 and 8

Borders

Trim the quilt top to 20" x 30". Referring to "Borders with Mitered Corners" on page 11, add the ¾"-wide and 5"-wide border strips to the quilt top.

Finishing

Mark the quilt top for quilting. Layer with backing fabric and batting. Baste, quilt, bind, and then label your Cinderella quilt.

Quilting Plan

Pegasus

Finished
size
32" x 32"

Color
photo
page 17

PEGASUS FLEW over Corinth, saw the clear spring that Sisyphus had won from the river-god, and stopped to drink.
Ingri and Edgar Parin d'Aulaire † *Book of Greek Myths*

MATERIALS

Fabric (44" wide)	Pieces to Cut	Fabric (44" wide)	Pieces to Cut
1 yd. dark blue	27" x 27" sky background	¼ yd. for first border	4 strips, each ¾" x 42"
½ yd. pale blue	Clouds 1–5	¼ yd. for second border	4 strips, each 1¾" x 42"
¼ yd. bright blue	Ocean	¼ yd. for third border	4 strips, each 2¾" x 42"
¼ yd. white	Pegasus, wings 1 & 2, tail, mane, forelock	1½ yds. for backing and binding	
Assorted scraps	Legs 1 & 2, moon, land 1–3	40" x 40" piece of batting	
1 yd. frame fabric	27" x 27"	Black fine-line permanent marker	

Instructions

Referring to "Appliquéing the Pieces" on pages 8–9, prepare the templates and appliqué pieces.

1. Fold the background fabric in half and in half again; then press gently to mark the center. Unfold the fabric and align the creases with the center lines on the pattern. Transfer pattern lines to the background fabric for appliqué placement.

2. Appliqué the pieces to the background in the following order:
   Clouds 1 and 2
   Ocean
   Land 1–3
   Clouds 3–5

3. Referring to "Adding Details with Markers" on page 10, use the black marker to draw details on the horse's mane and tail.

4. Appliqué the remaining pieces to the background in the following order:
   Mane, tail, wing 1
   Legs 1 and 2
   Pegasus body
   Forelock, wing 2
   Moon

5. Referring to "Framing a Circular Design" on page 10, trace the pattern circle onto the frame fabric and reverse-appliqué it to the background fabric. Trim the background fabric behind the frame fabric, leaving a ⅜"-wide seam allowance.

Borders

Trim the quilt top to 26" x 26". Referring to "Borders with Straight-Cut Corners" on page 12, add the ¾"-wide border strips, the 1¾"-wide border strips, and then the 2¾"-wide border strips.

Finishing

Mark the quilt top for quilting. Layer with backing fabric and batting. Baste, quilt, bind, and then label your Pegasus quilt.

Quilting Plan

Dragonslayer

Finished
size
26" x 36"

Color
photo
page 18

MATERIALS

Fabric (44" wide)	Pieces to Cut
¾ yd. blue	21" x 32" sky background
⅓ yd. dark blue #1	Clouds 1 & 3
⅛ yd. dark blue #2	Spires 1–3
¼ yd. medium blue #1	Cloud 2
⅛ yd. medium blue #2	Cliffs 2 & 6
⅛ yd. tan	Land 1
⅛ yd. orchid	Land 2
⅛ yd. light tan	Land 3
⅛ yd. mauve	Cliffs 1 & 4
¼ yd. rust	Cliffs 3 & 5
⅛ yd. medium gold	Land 4
⅛ yd. dark gold	Land 5
7" x 9" black	Horse
¼ yd. green print	Dragon 2 & 4, legs 1 & 2, wing 8, wing 14, tail 2

Fabric (44" wide)	Pieces to Cut
⅛ yd. print	Dragon 1, tail 1 & 3
¼ yd. assorted tans	Wings 1–7 & 9–13
Assorted scraps	Horse mane and tail, horse mantle, knight, shield, bridle, dragon 3, horns*, eye*
⅛ yd. for first border	4 strips, each ¾" x 42"
½ yd. for second border	4 strips, each 3½" x 42"
1¼ yds. for backing and binding	
30" x 40" piece of batting	

Black embroidery floss

Black and red permanent fine-line markers
*Ultra Suede optional

Instructions

Referring to "Appliquéing the Pieces" on pages 8–9, prepare the templates and appliqué pieces using the pullout pattern.

1. Fold the background fabric in half and in half again; then press gently to mark the center. Unfold the fabric and align the creases with the center lines on the pattern. Transfer pattern lines to the background fabric for appliqué placement.

2. Appliqué the pieces to the background in the following order:
   Clouds 1–3
   Spires 1–3
   Land 1–3
   Cliffs 1–6
   Land 4 and 5
   Mane, tail, horse, mantle, bridle, knight, shield
   Dragon wings 1–8
   Dragon legs 1 and 2, horn 1, body 1–4, horn 2, leg 3
   Dragon tail 1–3, wings 9–14
   Eye of dragon (appliqué or embroider)

3. Referring to "Adding Details with Markers" on page 10, lightly draw reins, lance, and stirrup with the black fine-line marker; then carefully stipple around the dragon's eye. Draw the nostril, 4 teeth, and the pupil in the eye. With the red fine-line marker, color the dragon's tongue.

Borders

Trim the quilt top to 20" x 30". Referring to "Borders with Mitered Corners" on page 11, add the ¾"-wide and 3½"-wide border strips to the quilt top.

Finishing

Mark the quilt top for quilting. Layer with backing fabric and batting. Baste, quilt, bind, and then label your Dragonslayer quilt.

Quilting Plan

"AS SOON AS you are fifteen," said their grandmother, "you will all be allowed to rise up above the water and sit on the rocks in the moonlight to watch the big ships sail by."

Hans Christian Andersen † *The Little Mermaid*

The Little Mermaid

Finished
size
30" x 35"

Color
photo
page 19

MATERIALS

Fabric (44" wide)	Pieces to Cut	Fabric (44" wide)	Pieces to Cut
½ yd. sky print	10" x 25" sky background	¼ yd. white (first border)	Sails 1–6* 4 strips, each ¾" x 42"
⅝ yd. water print	16" x 25" ocean background	2 yds. border print (second border)	2 strips, each 5" x 42"; cut on lengthwise grain
⅓ yd. *each* of 2 blues	Clouds 1–4		2 strips, each 5" x 48"; cut on lengthwise grain
¼ yd. wave print	Waves 1 & 2	1⅜ yds. for backing and binding	
¼ yd. dark gray	Rocks 1–3	34" x 39" piece of batting	
⅛ yd. medium gray	Dolphins 1–4		
10" x 10" green	Mermaid tail	Black fine-line permanent marker	
Assorted scraps	Mermaid body, left arm, hair, land 1–3, ship	*Ultra Suede optional	

Instructions

Copy the pattern sections from pages 46–52 onto a large sheet of paper, referring to the Section Guide on page 52.

Referring to "Appliquéing the Pieces" on pages 8–9, prepare the templates and appliqué pieces.

1. Transfer the necessary pattern lines to the sky background, and appliqué the pieces to it in the following order:
   Clouds 1–4
   Land 1 and 2
2. Referring to "Adding Details with Markers" on page 10, mark the ship's masts and flags on the sky fabric with the black marker. Then appliqué the ship and sails to the sky.
3. Sew the sky and water backgrounds together. Press the seam toward the water fabric.
4. Fold the sky/water background in half and in half again; then press gently to mark the center. Unfold the fabric and align the creases with the center lines on the pattern. Transfer pattern lines to the background fabric for appliqué placement.
5. Appliqué the pieces to the background in the following order:
   Land 3
   Dolphins 1–4
   Rocks 1–3
   Wave 1
6. Use the black marker to draw details on the mermaid's hair, and mark the appropriate features on the mermaid's face and on dolphin 4.
7. Appliqué the remaining pieces in the following order:
   Mermaid body, tail
   Mermaid hair
   Mermaid left arm
   Wave 2

Borders

Trim the quilt top to 20" x 24". Referring to "Borders with Mitered Corners" on page 11, add the ¾"-wide and 5"-wide border strips to the quilt top.

Finishing

Mark the quilt top for quilting. Layer with backing fabric and batting. Baste, quilt, bind, and then label your Little Mermaid quilt.

Quilting Plan

WHEN THEY WERE quite near they saw that the cottage was made of gingerbread and covered with cakes, while the windows were made of transparent sugar.

Jakob and Wilhelm Grimm † *Hansel and Gretel*

Hansel and Gretel

Finished
size
32" x 27"

Color
photo
page 20

MATERIALS

Fabric (44" wide)	Pieces to Cut	Fabric (44" wide)	Pieces to Cut
½ yd. blue	12" x 27" sky background	Assorted scraps	Chimney, gumdrops*, mullions*, window trim*; arms 2 & 3, neck 2, dress, belt, hair, bows*; arms 1 & 2, neck 1, hair, shirt, straps 1 & 2, pants; witch's face, hat, dress; steps
½ yd. light brown print	10" x 27" path background		
¼ yd. *each* of 9 green prints	Land 3–9, tree tops 1 & 2, bushes 1–4, evergreens 1 & 2		
¼ yd. floral print	Land 1 & 2	¼ yd. for first border	4 strips, each ¾" x 42"
⅓ yd. brown print	Tree trunks 1–4	¼ yd. for second border	4 strips, each 1¼" x 42"
¼ yd. red-and-white stripe	Candy canes 1–8	⅜ yd. for third border	4 strips, each 3" x 42"
¼ yd. dark brown	Windows 1–3, door	1⅜ yds. for backing and batting	
¼ yd. pink	Roof & chimney icings	36" x 31" piece of batting	
9" x 12" tan	Gingerbread house	Black and brown fine-line permanent markers	
Scraps of lace	Window & door trims	*Ultra Suede optional	

Instructions

Referring to "Appliquéing the Pieces" on pages 8–9, prepare the templates and appliqué pieces using the pullout pattern.

1. Mark the necessary pattern lines on the sky background and appliqué the pieces in the following order:

   Evergreens 1 and 2

   Tree trunk 1

   Bushes 1–4

   Gingerbread house, chimney, windows, mullions, window trim, door, door trim, house trim, candy canes 1–8, roof icing, roof gumdrops, chimney icing, chimney gumdrop

2. Sew the path background to the appliquéd sky using a ¼"-wide seam allowance. Press the seam toward the path.

3. Fold the background fabric in half and in half again; then press gently to mark the center. Unfold the fabric and align the creases with the center lines on the pattern. Transfer pattern lines to the background fabric for appliqué placement.

4. Appliqué the remaining pieces to the background in the following order:

   Land 1–9 (Leave section of seam between land 5 and 7 unsewn.)

   Steps 1 and 2

   Witch's dress, face, and hat

   Tree trunks 2–4 (Tuck the bottom of tree 4 between lands 5 and 7; then appliqué the opening closed.)

   Treetops 1 and 2

   Hansel's arms 1 and 2, neck 1, hair, shirt, straps 1 & 2, and pants (topstitch pants details)

   Gretel's arms 3 and 4, neck 2, dress, belt, hair, and bows

5. Referring to "Adding Details with Markers" on page 10, use the black and brown markers to add features to the witch's face and details to the children's hair.

Borders

Trim the quilt top to 20" x 26". Referring to "Borders with Straight-Cut corners" on page 12, add the ¾"-wide border strips, the 1¼"-wide border strips, and then the 3"-wide border strips.

Finishing

Mark the quilt top for quilting. Layer with backing fabric and batting. Baste, quilt, bind, and then label your Hansel and Gretel quilt.

Quilting Plan

The Unicorns

Finished
size
31" x 31"

Color
photo
page 21

MATERIALS

Fabric (44" wide)	Pieces to Cut	Fabric (44" wide)	Pieces to Cut
⅝ yd. light blue	15½" x 27" sky background	Scrap of gray	Legs 1 & 2
½ yd. medium blue	12½" x 27" water background	1 yd. frame fabric	28" x 28"
¼ yd. *each* of 4 greens	Bushes 1–3, tree tops 1–5	¼ yds. for first border	4 strips, each ¾" x 42"
½ yd. brown	Tree trunks 1–3	⅛ yd. for second border	4 strips, each 1½" x 42"
⅛ yd. *each* of 3 earth tones	Land 1–3	¼ yd. for third border	4 strips, each 2¼" x 42"
¼ yd. white	Unicorns 1 & 2, manes 1 & 2, tails 1 & 2, horns 1 & 2	1⅜" yd. for backing and binding	
		35" x 35" piece of batting	

Black and gray fine-line permanent markers

Instructions

Trace the pattern sections from the pullouts onto a large sheet of paper.

Referring to "Appliquéing the Pieces" on pages 8–9, prepare the templates and appliqué pieces.

1. Sew the sky and water fabrics together along the 27"-long edges to make the background. Press the seam toward the water.
2. Fold the background fabric in half and in half again; then press gently to mark the center. Unfold the fabric and align the creases with the center lines on the pattern. Transfer pattern lines to the background fabric for appliqué placement.
3. Appliqué the pieces to the background in the following order:
   Bushes 1 and 2
   Tree trunk 1
   Land 1
   Tree trunks 2 and 3
   Treetops 1–5
   Land 2 and 3
   Bush 3
   Horn 1, tail 1, leg 1, mane 1, unicorn 1
   Leg 2, mane 2, tail 2, unicorn 2, horn 2

   Notice that you must appliqué the forelock of each unicorn's mane over the unicorn's body and the remainder underneath. Also, part of unicorn 2's tail lies under the body and part on top.
4. Referring to "Adding Details with Markers" on page 10, use the gray marker to color the unicorns' manes and tails if desired. Use the black marker to add the eyes and nostrils.
5. Referring to "Framing a Circular Design" on page 10, fold the frame fabric in half and in half again; then press gently to mark the center. Trace the 20½" pattern circle on the front of the frame fabric. Leaving a ³⁄₁₆"-wide seam allowance, cut away the center of the circle. Align the frame fabric over the design area and reverse-appliqué the frame fabric to the scene, turning under the circle line. Leaving a ³⁄₈"-wide seam allowance around the circle, trim the design area behind the frame fabric, and then press.

Borders

Trim the quilt top to 26" x 26". Referring to "Borders with Straight-Cut Corners" on page 12, add the ¾"-wide border strips, the 1½"-wide border strips, and then the 2¼"-wide border strips.

Finishing

Mark the quilt top for quilting. Layer with backing fabric and batting. Baste, quilt, bind, and then label your Unicorn quilt.

Quilting Plan

THEN SHE PUT twenty mattresses on top of the pea and twenty eiderdown quilts on top
of the mattresses. And this was the bed in which the Princess was to spend the night.

Hans Christian Andersen † *The Princess and the Pea*

The Princess and the Pea

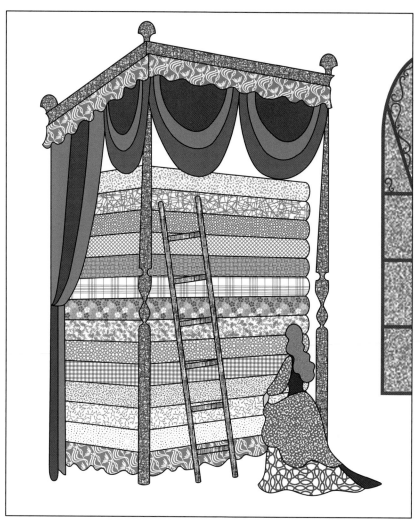

Finished
size
29" x 33"

Color
photo
page 22

MATERIALS

Fabric (44" wide)	Pieces to Cut	Fabric (44" wide)	Pieces to Cut
¾ yd. off-white	21" x 25" (background)	⅛ yd. brown	Ladder
⅛ yd. print	Bed valance 1 & 1a, bed skirt 1 & 1a	Assorted scraps	Mattresses 1–13, dress, hair, hands
⅛ yd. blue	Window	¼ yd. for first border	4 strips, each ¾" x 42"
¼ yd. light purple	Swags 1a–3a,	¼ yd. for second border	4 strips, each 1½" x 42"
¼ yd. medium purple	Swags 1–3, curtains 2, 3, 5	¼ yd. for third border	4 strips, each 1" x 42"
¼ yd. dark purple	Swags 1b–3b, curtains 1 & 4	⅜ yd. for fourth border	4 strips, each 3" x 42"
¼ yd. gold metallic	Bed tops 1 & 1a, posts 1 & 2, finials 1–3	Black medium-line and fine-line permanent markers	

Instructions

Trace the pattern sections from pages 53–59 onto a large sheet of paper using the Section Guide on page 59.

Referring to "Appliquéing the Pieces" on pages 8–9, prepare the templates and appliqué pieces.

1. Fold the background fabric in half and in half again; then press gently to mark the center. Unfold the fabric and align the creases with the center lines on the pattern. Transfer pattern lines to the background fabric for appliqué placement.

2. Appliqué the pieces to the background in the following order:
   Mattresses 1–13
   Bed skirts 1 and 1a
   Curtains 1–5
   Posts 1 and 2
   Swags 1, 1a, 1b, 2, 2a, 2b, 3, 3a, and 3b
   Finials 1–3
   Bed tops 1 and 1a
   Valance 1 and 1a
   Princess 1–7
   Ladder
   Window (Before appliquéing, mark the window with the black markers as indicated on the pattern. Refer to "Adding Details with Markers" on page 10.)

Borders

Trim the quilt top to 20" x 24". Referring to "Borders with Straight-Cut Corners" on page 12, add the ¾"-wide border strips, the 1½"-wide border strips, the 1"-wide border strips, and then the 3"-wide border strips.

Finishing

Mark the quilt top for quilting. Layer with backing fabric and batting. Baste, quilt, bind, and then label your Princess and the Pea quilt.

Quilting Plan

ONE EVENING, when the sun was setting in all its splendor, a large flock of big hand-
some birds came out of the bushes. The Duckling had never before seen anything quite
so beautiful as they were–dazzlingly white, with long supple necks–they were swans!

Hans Christian Andersen † *The Ugly Duckling*

The Ugly Duckling

Finished
size
33" x 33"

Color
photo
page 23

MATERIALS

Fabric (44" wide)	Pieces to Cut	Fabric (44" wide)	Pieces to Cut
⅝ yd. blue	17" x 29" for sky background	Assorted scraps	Duckling 1, 2 & 4, cattails 1–7
½ yd. blue-green	13½" x 29" for water background	1 yd. frame fabric	29" x 29"
¼ yd. pink or peach	Clouds 1–3	⅛ yd. for first border	4 strips, each 1½" x 42"
⅛ yd. brown or gold	Land 1 & 2	¼ yd. for second border	4 strips, each 2¼" x 42"
¼ yd. *each* of 3 greens	Leaves 1–11, stems 1–6	1½ yds. for backing and binding	
¼ yd. white	Swans 1–3, wings 1 & 2	37" x 37" piece of batting	
9" x 9" gray print	Duckling 3	Black and orange fine-line permanent markers	

Instructions

Referring to "Appliquéing the Pieces" on pages 8–9, prepare the templates and appliqué pieces using the pullout pattern.

1. Sew the sky and water backgrounds together along the 29"-long edges, using a ¼"-wide seam allowance. Press the seam toward the water.

2. Align the pattern and background using the fold marks and transfer the necessary pattern lines to the background fabric.

3. Appliqué pieces to the background in the following order:
   Clouds 1–3
   Land 1 and 2
   Wing 1
   Swans 1–3
   Wing 2
   Stems 1–7, cattails 1–7
   Leaves 1–10
   Duckling 1–4
   Leaf 11

4. Fold the frame fabric in half and in half again; then press gently to mark the center. Referring to "Framing a Circular Design" on page 10, appliqué the frame fabric to the design area. Trim the design area behind the frame fabric around the circle, leaving a ⅜"-wide seam allowance.

5. Referring to "Adding Details with Markers" on page 10, draw the duckling's eye and nostril, swans' muzzles, cattail tips, and distant islands with the black marker. Draw bills on the swans with the orange marker.

Borders

Trim the quilt top to 28" x 28". Referring to "Borders with Straight-Cut Corners" on page 12, add the 1½"-wide border strips and the 2¼"-wide border strips.

Finishing

Mark the quilt top for quilting. Layer with backing fabric and batting. Baste, quilt, bind, and then label your Ugly Duckling quilt.

Quilting Plan

WHENEVER SHE HEARD the witch's voice she loosened her braids and let her hair fall down out
of the window. This became a ladder for the old witch to climb straight up to the top of the tower.

Jakob and Wilhelm Grimm † *Rapunzel*

Rapunzel

Finished
size
28" x 36"

Color
photo
page 24

MATERIALS

Fabric (44" wide)	Pieces to Cut	Fabric (44" wide)	Pieces to Cut
¾ yd. dark blue	21" x 29" for sky background	Assorted scraps	Rocks 1–4, roofs 1–3, braces 1 & 2, windows 1–4, bridge 1 & 2, Rapunzel, witch
⅓ yd. light blue	Clouds 1–3		
⅛ yd. tan	Towers 1 & 2		
½ yd. brown print #1	Towers 3 & 4	¼ yd. for first border	4 strips, each ¾" x 42"
¼ yd. brown print #2	Tree	¼ yd. for second border	4 strips, each 1½" x 42"
¼ yd. green #1	Bushes 1–3	⅓ yd. print for third border	4 strips, each 3" x 42"
¼ yd. green #2	Land 1	1¼ yds. for backing and binding	
¼ yd. green #3	Land 2	32" x 40" piece of batting	
⅛ yd. yellow	Hair	Black fine-line permanent marker	

Instructions

Referring to "Appliquéing the Pieces" on pages 8–9, prepare the templates and appliqué pieces using the pullout pattern.

1. Fold the background fabric in half and in half again; then press gently to mark the center. Unfold the fabric and align the creases with the center lines on the pattern. Transfer pattern lines to the background fabric for appliqué placement.

2. Appliqué the pieces to the background in the following order:
   Clouds 1–3
   Bushes 1 and 2
   Bridge 1 and 2
   Braces 1 and 2, towers 1 and 2,
     roof 1 and 2, windows 1 and 2
   Tower 3, roof 3, window 3
   Tower 4, window 4
   Bush 3
   Land 1
   Rocks 1 and 2
   Land 2
   Rocks 3 and 4
   Tree
   Rapunzel, hair
   Witch

Borders

Trim the quilt top to 20" x 28". Referring to "Borders with Straight-Cut Corners" on page 12 add the ¾"-wide border strips, the 1½"-wide border strips, and then the 3"-wide border strips.

Finishing

Mark the quilt top for quilting. Layer with backing fabric and batting. Baste, quilt, bind, and then label your Rapunzel quilt.

Quilting Plan

"FAREWELL, dear good little girl!" said the Swallow, and flew off into the sunshine.
Thumbelina gazed after him with tears in her eyes, for she was very fond of the Swallow.

Hans Christian Andersen † *Thumbelina*

Thumbelina

Finished
size
31" x 31"

Color
photo
page 25

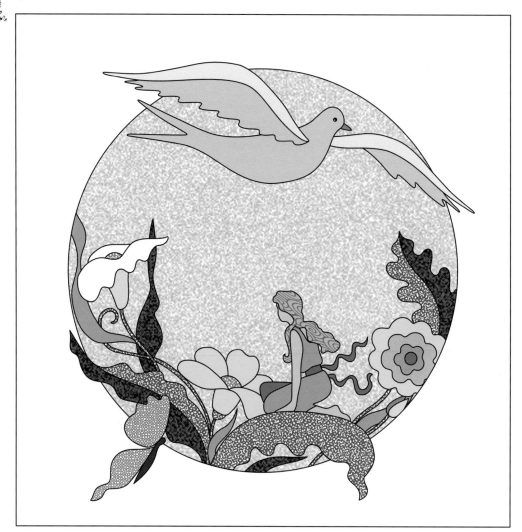

MATERIALS

Fabric (44" wide)	Pieces to Cut	Fabric (44" wide)	Pieces to Cut
1 yd. blue	28" x 28" for sky background	1 yd. frame fabric	28" x 28"
¼ yd. *each* of 3 greens	Leaf 1–10, stem 1–5, calyx	⅛ yd. for first border	4 strips, each ¾" x 42"
⅛ yd. light gold	Bird	¼ yd. for second border	4 strips, each 3¼" x 42"
⅛ yd. tan	Wings 1 & 2	1½ yds. for backing and binding	
⅛ yd. white	Wings 3 & 4	36" x 36" piece of batting	
Assorted scraps	Flowers 1–17, butterfly 1–3; Thumbelina's body, leg, knee, dress, sash, ribbons, & hair; beak*	Black fine-line permanent marker
*Ultra Suede optional	

Instructions

Trace the pattern sections from pages 60–66 onto a large sheet of paper using the Section Guide on page 66.

Referring to "Appliquéing the Pieces" on pages 8–9, prepare the templates and appliqué pieces.

1. Fold the background fabric in half and in half again; then press gently to mark the center. Unfold the fabric and align the creases with the center lines on the pattern. Transfer pattern lines to the background fabric for appliqué placement.

2. Appliqué the pieces to the background in the following order:
   Leaves 1, 2, and 3
   Stems 1 and 2
   Flowers 1–6
   Leaf 4 (Appliqué only the base of leaf 4, which extends under stem 3, until after stem 4 has been appliquéd.)
   Leaf 5
   Stem 3, stem 4 (After appliquéing stem 4, finish appliquéing leaf 4.)
   Flowers 7–10
   Stem 5
   Leaf 6, leaf 7 (Leave tip unsewn until after the frame has been appliquéd.)
   Leaves 8 and 9
   Calyx, flowers 11–17
   Body (Leave arm unstitched until after the lower part of dress 1 has been appliquéd.)
   Knee, leg, ribbons 1 and 2, dress 1 and 2, hair, sash
   Leaf 10 (Leave tip unsewn until after the frame has been appliquéd.)

3. Referring to "Framing a Circular Design" on page 10, trace the 20½" circle onto the frame fabric and reverse appliqué it to the design area. Trim the design area behind the frame fabric around the circle, leaving a ⅜"-wide seam allowance.

4. Complete the appliqué in the following order:
   Leaf tips 7 and 10
   Beak, wing 2, wing 4, bird
   Wings 1 and 3
   Butterfly 1–3

5. Referring to "Adding Details with Markers" on page 10, use the black marker to draw the eye of the bird, and the antennae and eye of the butterfly.

Borders

Trim the quilt top to 27" x 27". Referring to "Borders with Mitered Corners" on pages 11–12, add the ¾"-wide and 3¼"-wide border strips to the quilt top.

Finishing

Mark the quilt top for quilting. Layer with backing fabric and batting. Baste, quilt, bind, and then label your Thumbelina quilt.

Quilting Plan

The Little Mermaid

Sky Background

Cloud 1

Cloud 2

Sail 3

Sail 6

Sail 2

Sail 5

Sail 1

Brown marker

The Little Mermaid

Cloud 4

Cloud 3

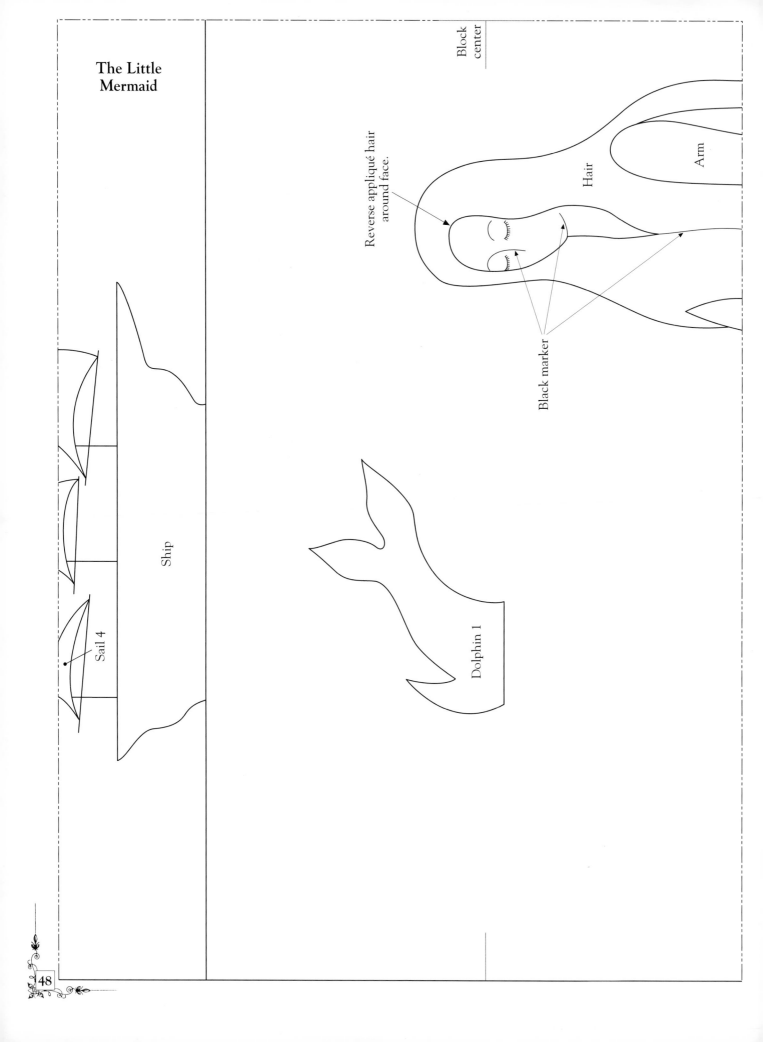

The Little Mermaid

Block center

Reverse appliqué hair around face.

Hair

Arm

Black marker

Ship

Sail 4

Dolphin 1

Block center

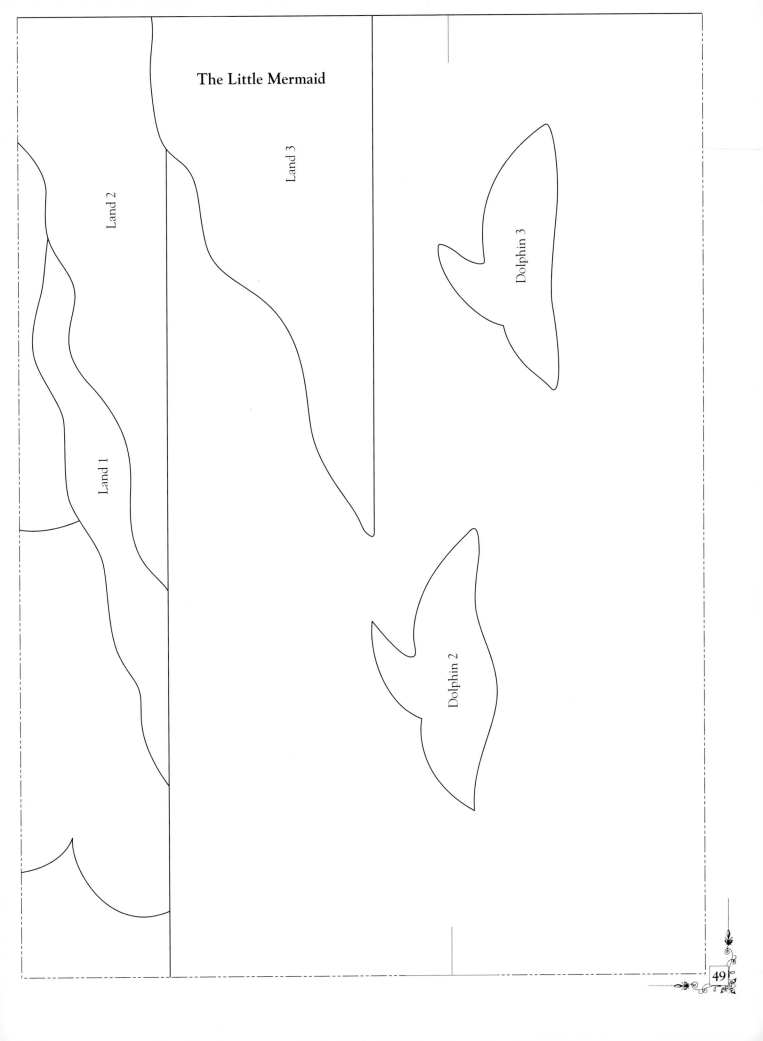

The Little Mermaid

Land 2

Land 3

Land 1

Dolphin 3

Dolphin 2

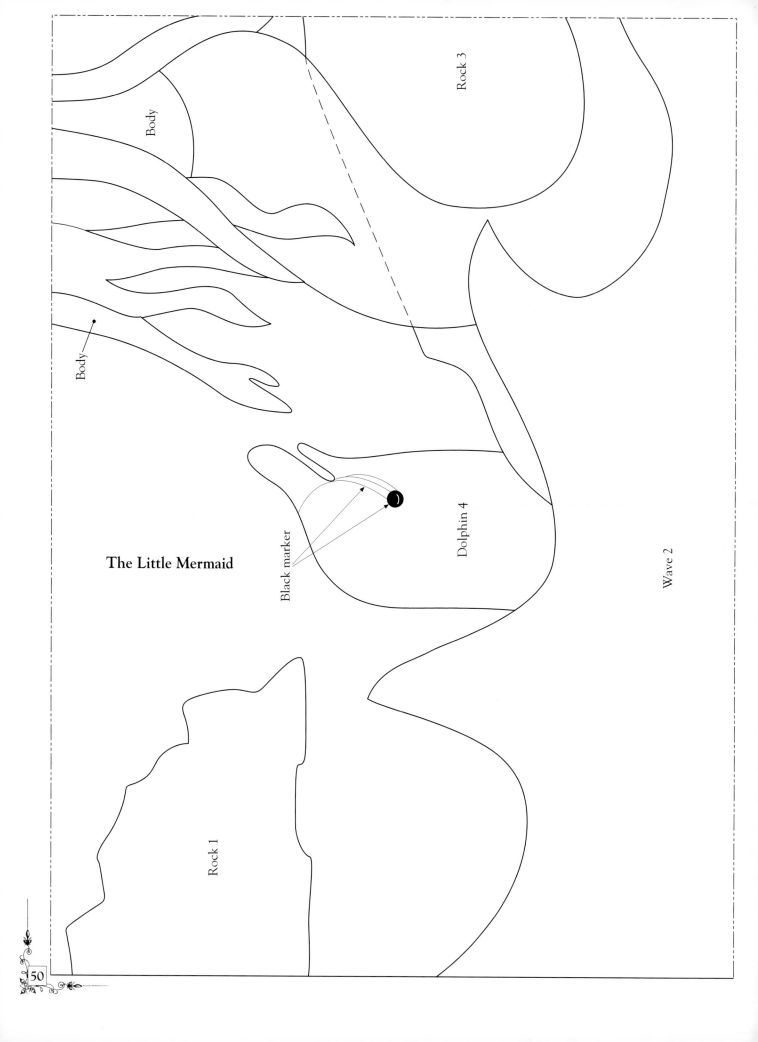

The Little Mermaid

Body

Body

Black marker

Rock 3

Dolphin 4

Wave 2

Rock 1

50

The Little Mermaid

Rock 2

Water Background

Tail

Wave 2

Wave 1

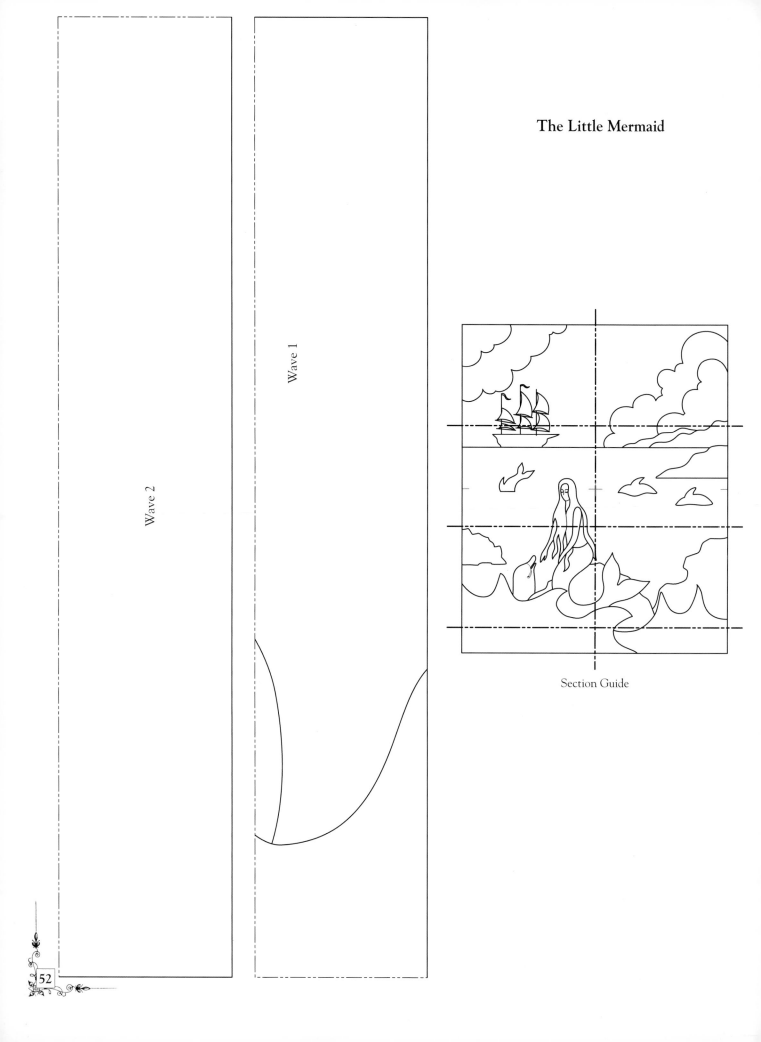

Section Guide

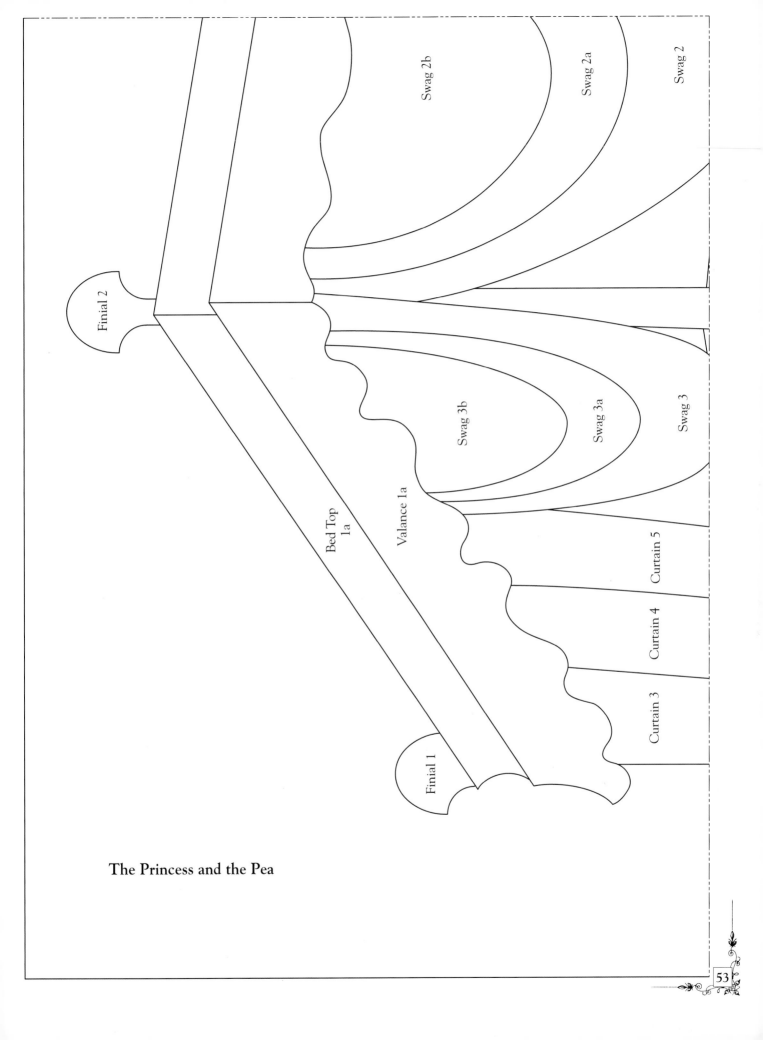

The Princess and the Pea

The Princess and the Pea

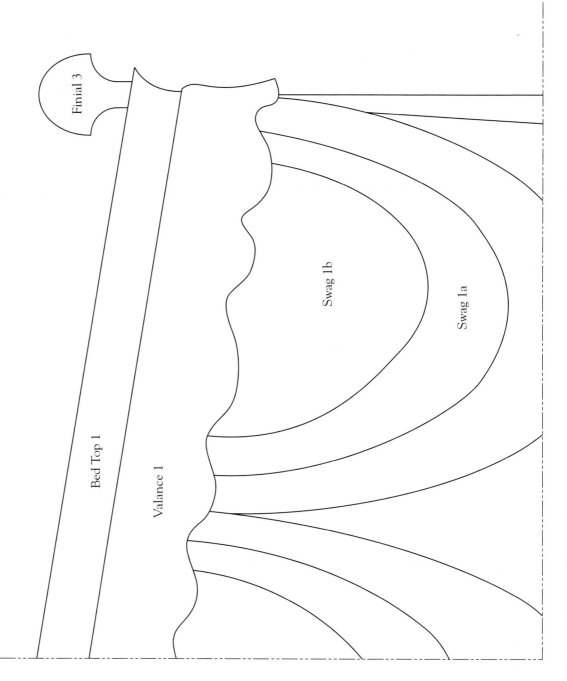

Finial 3

Bed Top 1

Valance 1

Swag 1b

Swag 1a

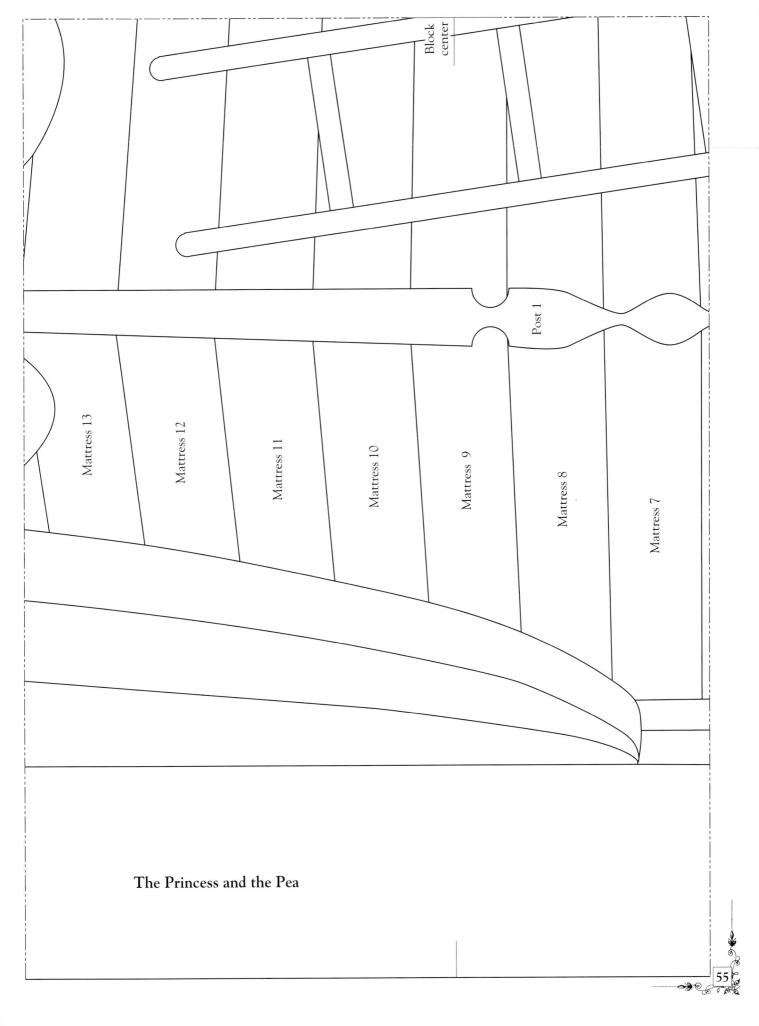

Block
center

Post 1

Mattress 13

Mattress 12

Mattress 11

Mattress 10

Mattress 9

Mattress 8

Mattress 7

The Princess and the Pea

Window

Black marker

The Princess and the Pea

Post 2

Swag 1

Ladder

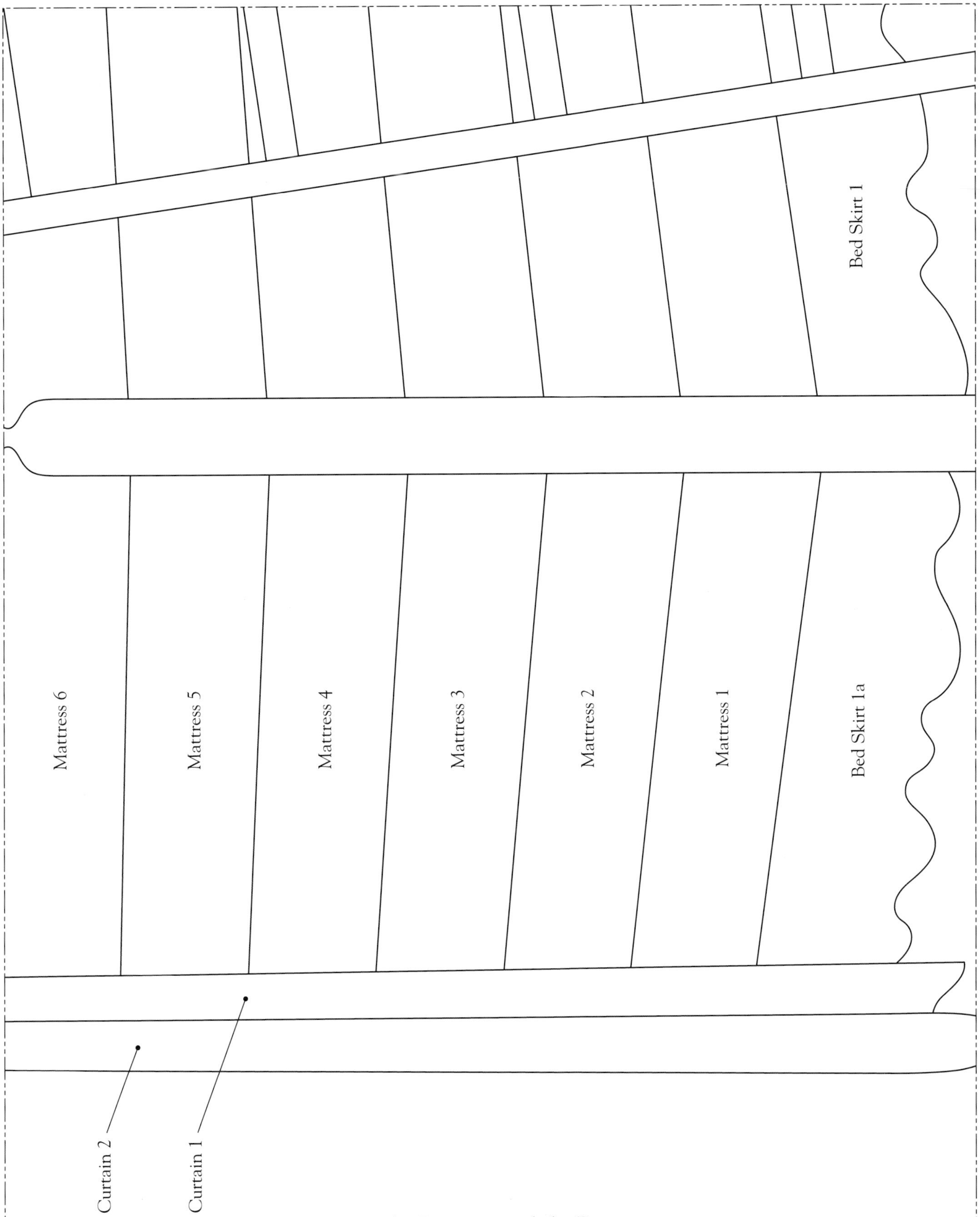

Bed Skirt 1

Mattress 6

Mattress 5

Mattress 4

Mattress 3

Mattress 2

Mattress 1

Bed Skirt 1a

Curtain 2

Curtain 1

The Princess and the Pea

The Princess and the Pea

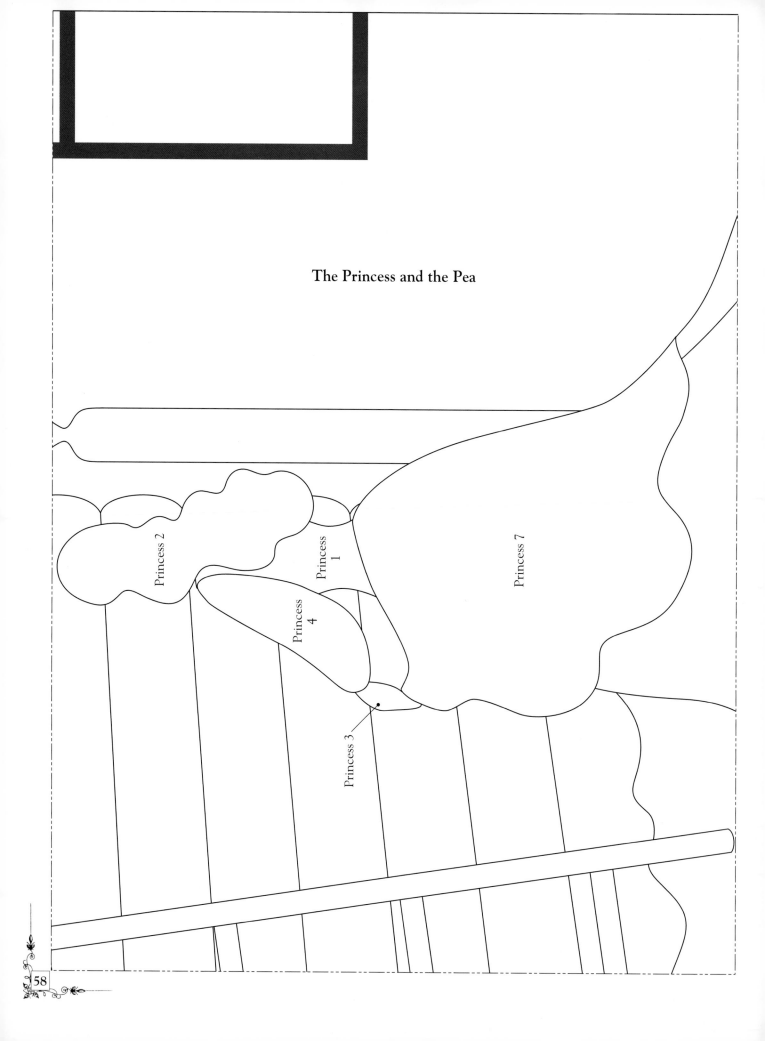

Princess 2

Princess 1

Princess 4

Princess 7

Princess 3

Princess 5

Princess 6

The Princess and the Pea

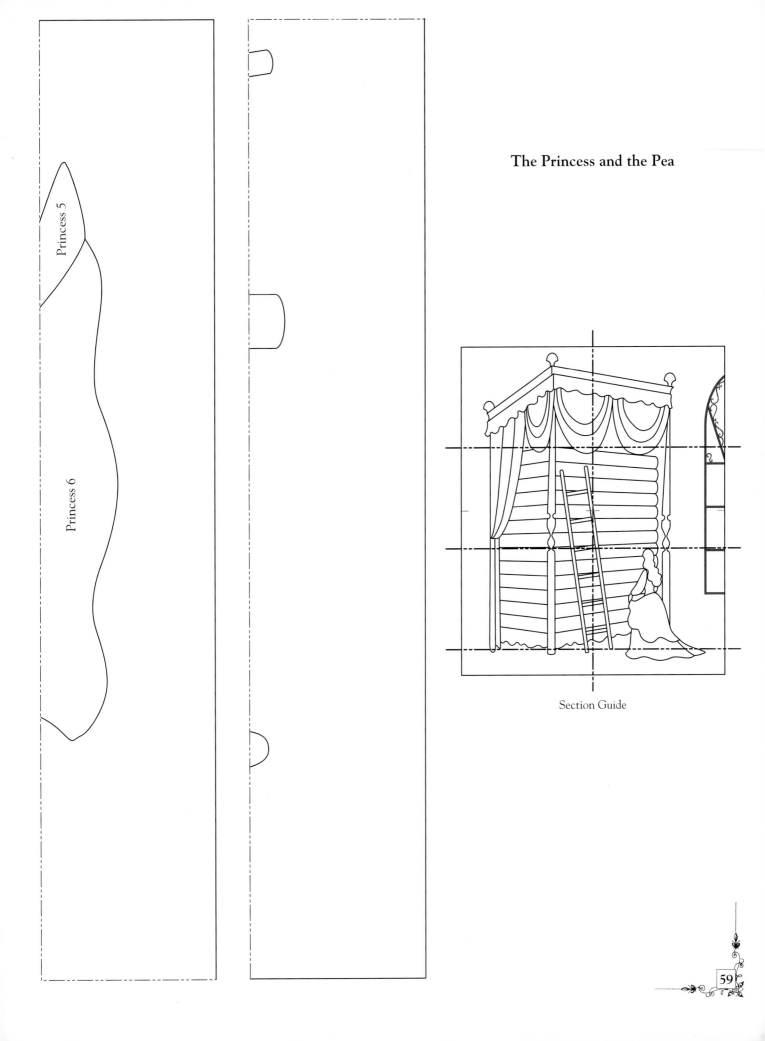

Section Guide

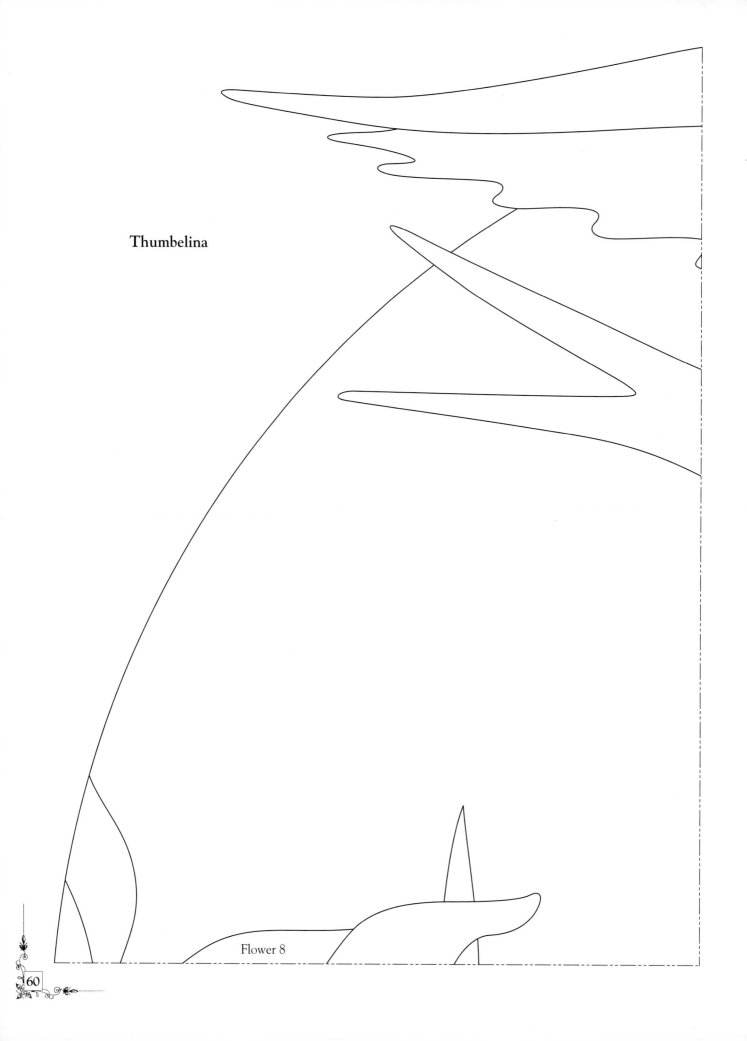

Thumbelina

Flower 8

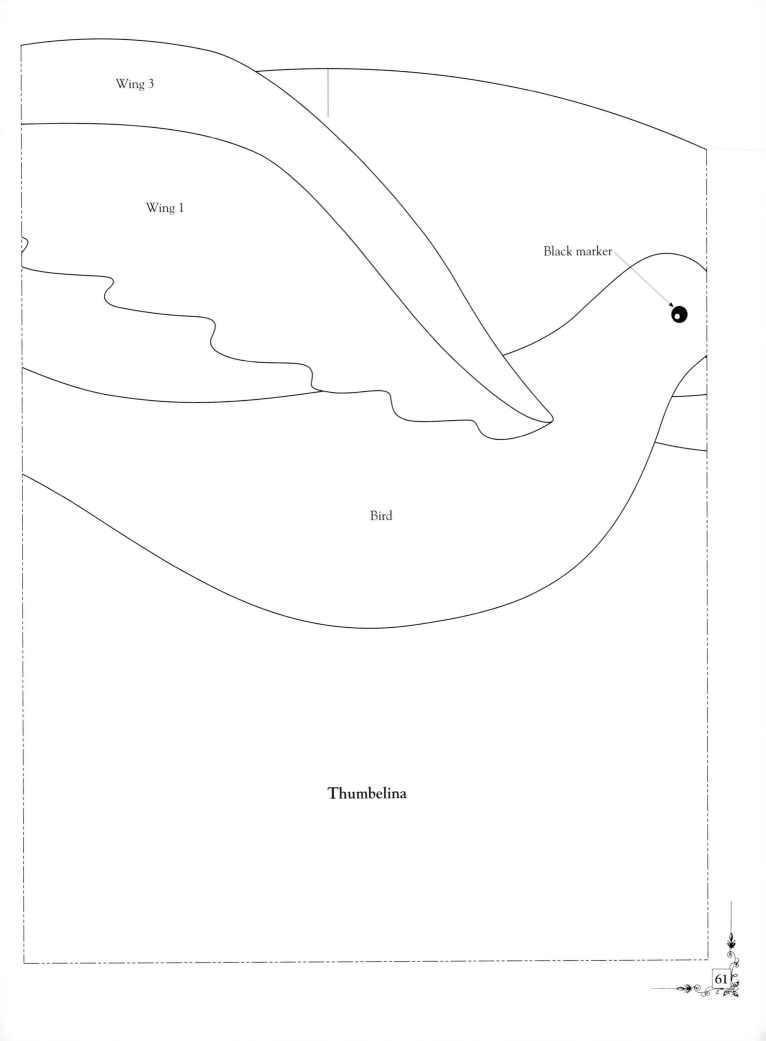

Wing 3

Wing 1

Black marker

Bird

Thumbelina

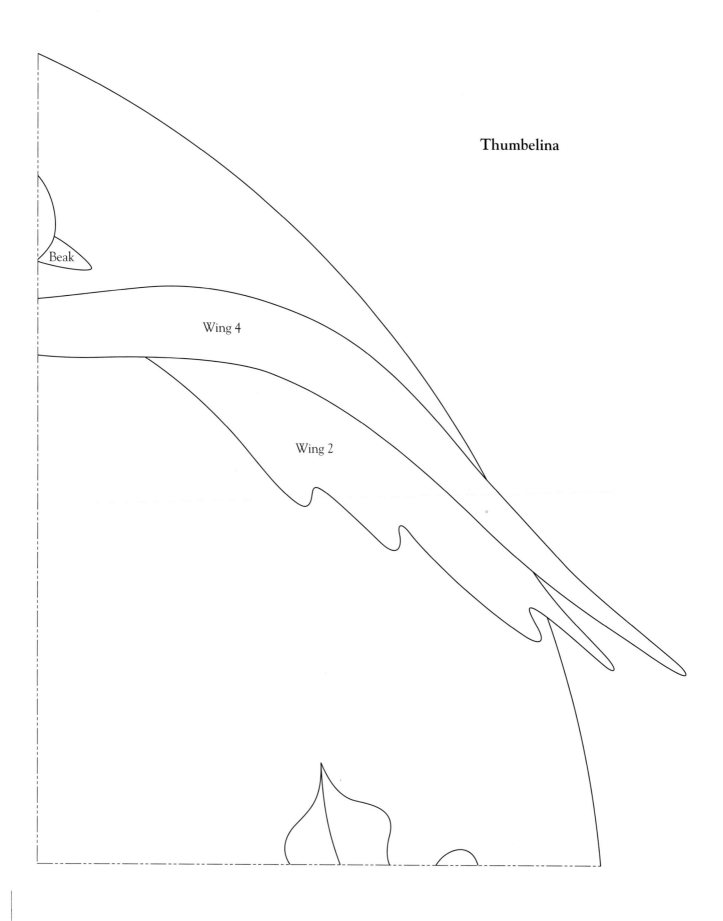

Thumbelina

Beak

Wing 4

Wing 2

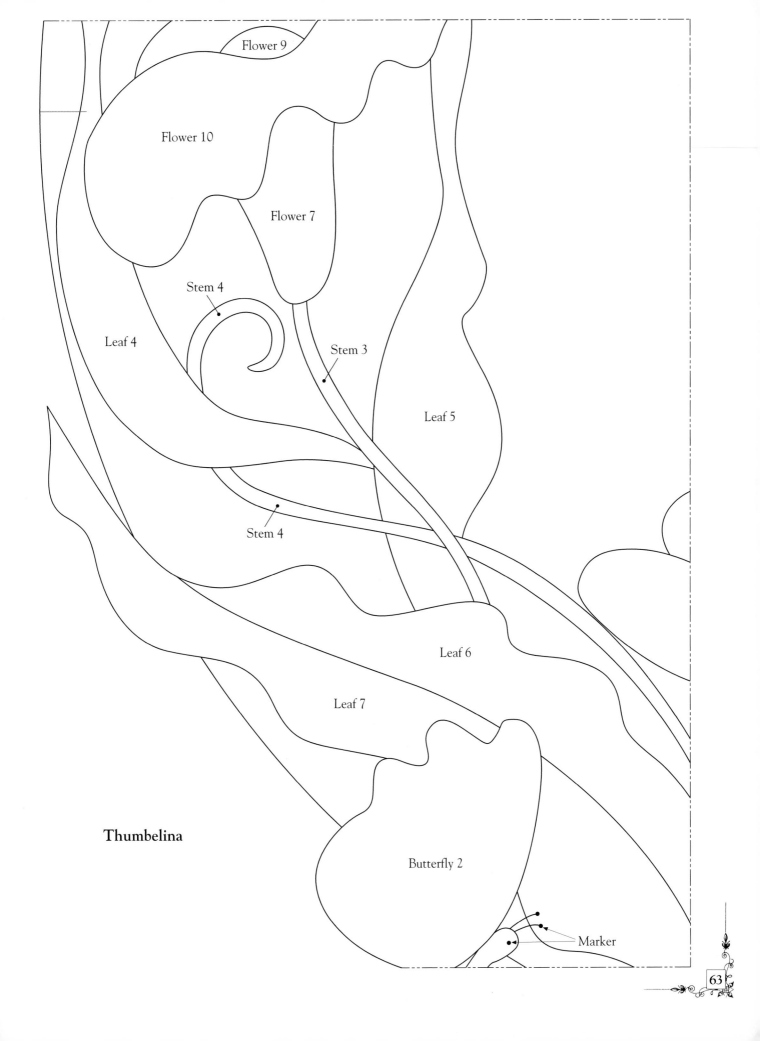

Flower 9

Flower 10

Flower 7

Stem 4

Leaf 4

Stem 3

Leaf 5

Stem 4

Leaf 6

Leaf 7

Thumbelina

Butterfly 2

Marker

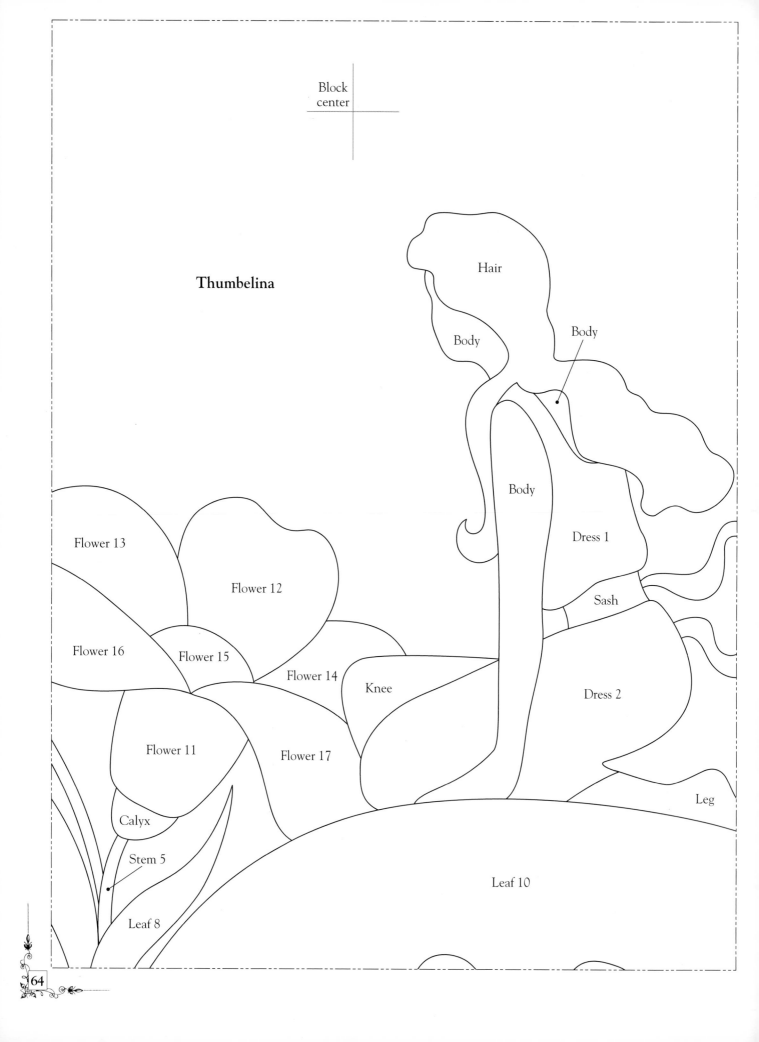

Block
center

Thumbelina

Hair

Body

Body

Body

Dress 1

Sash

Flower 13

Flower 12

Flower 16   Flower 15

Flower 14

Knee

Dress 2

Flower 11   Flower 17

Leg

Calyx

Stem 5

Leaf 10

Leaf 8

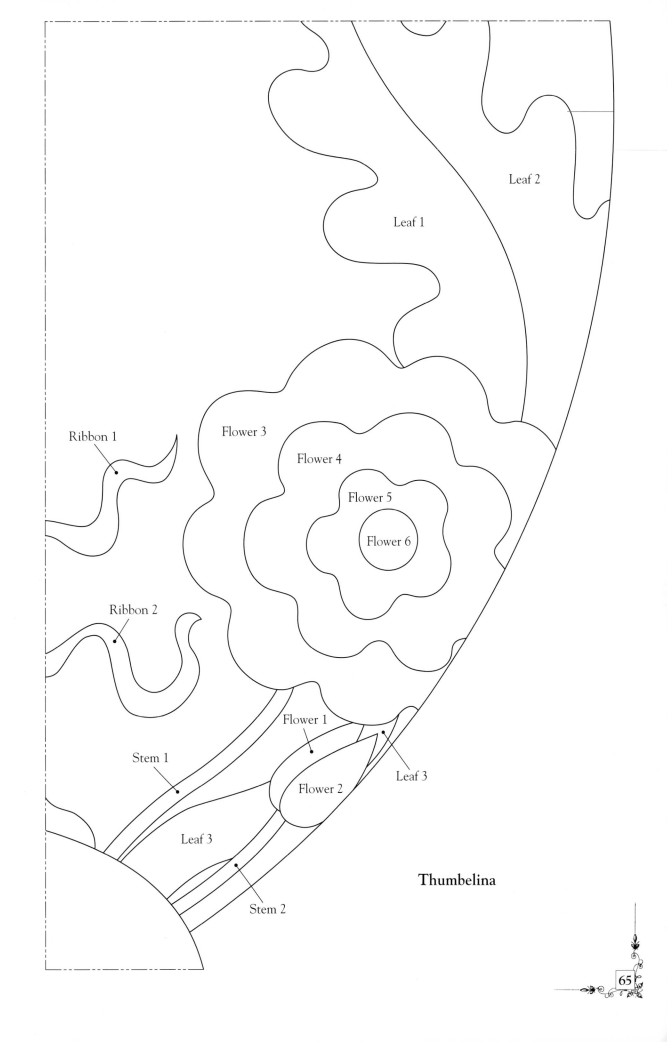

Leaf 2

Leaf 1

Ribbon 1

Flower 3

Flower 4

Flower 5

Flower 6

Ribbon 2

Flower 1

Stem 1

Leaf 3

Flower 2

Leaf 3

Thumbelina

Stem 2

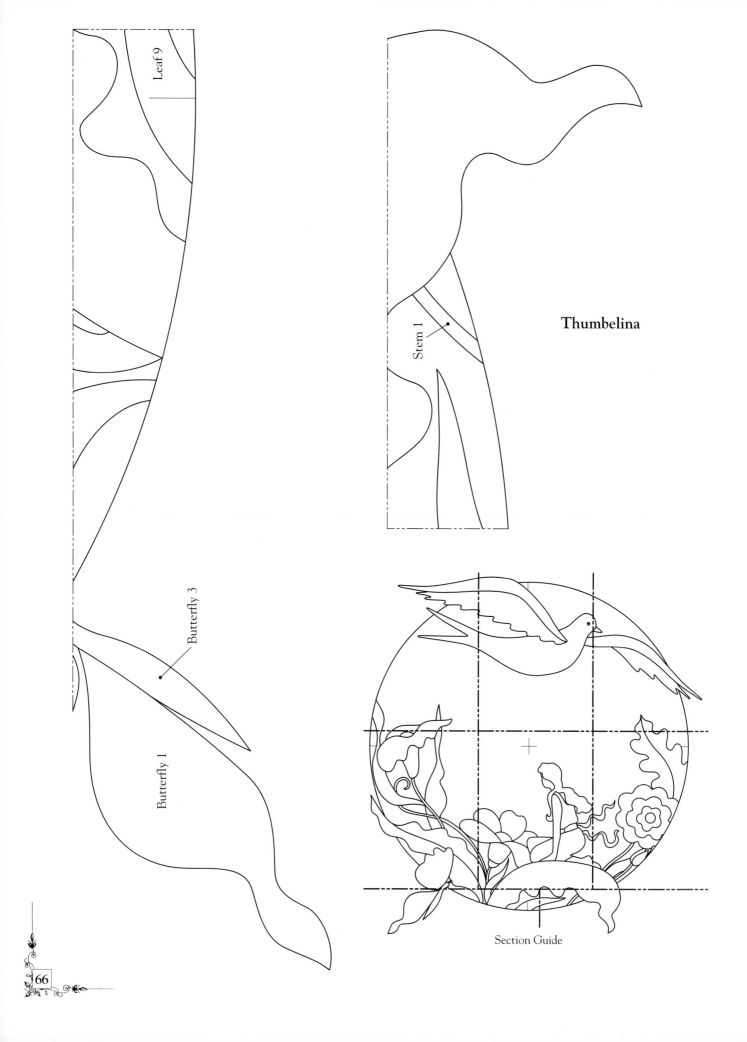

Leaf 9

Thumbelina

Stem 1

Butterfly 3

Butterfly 1

Section Guide

About the Authors

Photo by Turba Photography

Bonnie Kaster

BONNIE KASTER has been a quiltmaker and designer for fifteen years. With a background in art and fashion, Bonnie began by designing quilted jackets and vests. She has won many awards for her work, including the Staff's Choice Award in the 1992 Keepsake Quilting Challenge, and her designs have been featured on covers of the Keepsake Quilting catalogs. Since 1992, Bonnie and Virginia Athey, her partner in Sweet Memories Publishing, have produced and marketed more than fifty quilt patterns. Bonnie has been teaching classes based on her quilt patterns for the past three years.

An active member of Evergreen Quilters of Green Bay, Wisconsin, Bonnie lives with her husband, Paul, in DePere, Wisconsin. They have three grown children, Lisa, Dean, and Shana.

VIRGINIA ATHEY, Bonnie's friend and business partner, enabled Bonnie to publish this book by capturing her thoughts on a computer disk.

Publications and Products